Smith lets us overhear the private griefs and joys of immigrants old and new, of millwrights, coal miners, victims of floods; of college students; Vietnam-era survivors, of mothers, wives, and union women in what becomes a kind of chorus of working-class America. He stands on back stoops and front porches reading over the shoulders of folk caught up in the paradoxes of Americans "so lost and at home with their lives."
    ~Richard Hague, author of *Earnest Occupations*

Inspired by real lives and places.

In the grace of simple people we all learn to survive.

Other Books by Larry Smith

Fiction:

The Free Farm: A Novel (Bottom Dog Press, 2011).

The Long River Home: A Novel (Bottom Dog Press, 2009).

Faces and Voices: Tales (Bird Dog Publishing, 2007).

Working It Out (Ridgeway Press, 1998).

Beyond Rust (Bottom Dog Press, 1995).

Memoirs:

The Thick of Thin: Memoirs of a Working-Class Writer (Bottom Dog Press 2015).

Milldust and Roses (Ridgeway Press, 2002).

Poetry:

The Pears: Poems (Bottom Dog Press)

Lake Winds: Poems (Bottom Dog Press, 2014).

each moment all: Poems (March Street Press, 2011).

Tu Fu Comes to America: A Story in Poems (March Street Press 2010, rev. 2018).

A River Remains (WordTech Editions, 2006).

Thoreau's Lost Journal (Westron Press 2002, rev. 2017).

Steel Valley: Postcards & Letters (Pig Iron Press, 1992).

Across These States (Bottom Dog Press, 1985).

Scissors, Paper, Rock (Cleveland State University Poetry Center, 1982).

Echo Without Sound: Poems by Larry Smith, Etchings by Stephen Smigocki (Northwood Press, 1981).

Growth: Poems (Northwood Press, (1975).

Biography & Nonfiction:

Images of America: Mingo Junction, co-edited with Guy Mason (Arcadia Publishing, 2011).

Lawrence Ferlinghetti: Poet-At-Large (Southern Illinois University Press, 1983).

Kenneth Patchen: Rebel Poet in America (A Consortium of Small Presses, 2000; rev. 2013).

Films (Written and co-produced with Tom Koba):

James Wright's Ohio (1988).

Kenneth Patchen: An Art of Engagement (1989).

MINGO TOWN
&
MEMORIES

LARRY SMITH

BIRD DOG

PUBLISHING
Huron, Ohio

Credits

Cover Design by Susanna Sharp-Schwacke
Copy editing Ann Smith and Laura Smith
Cover Art: postcard from Madeline Brinski Campbell
& photo back cover by Ian Adams

Acknowledgments

First, I thank the people of Mingo Junction, Ohio, who lived and shared this world and many of these writings over the years—teachers, preachers, store owners, neighbors, and school friends. My writing career began in the 6th grade at the inspiration of Mrs. Ruth Merzi who handed us working-class kids small booklets of poems each week then went on to have us read and write poems of our own. I also thank the members of the Firelands Writing Center who shared these poems.

In a whole other realm, I owe so much to my family for sharing this life and my writing. My wife Ann (Zaben) Smith of Mingo has lived it and encouraged me for 50 years. There are so many good people and places in Mingo Junction that I hold deep in my mind and heart. These memories and places become stories. In some of theim Mingo speaks. I hope you enjoy some of these voices here.

Many of these poems have appeared in my books, including *Growth: Poems and Sketches, Ohio Zen: Inside the Garden, Milldust and Roses, A River Remains, Lake Winds,* and *The Pears.* Magazines have published this work in book or online format in *As It Ought to Be, Big Hammer, San Antonio Review, Pine Mountain, Sand and Gravel,* and more.

Contents

Mingo Town

Memories

Ohio Valley Steel Town (1960s)

Old store fronts
with new signs—
Green screen-doors boasting
of Wonder Bread
or Ne-Hi pop.

Cars double-park
in front of Islay's
while old men walk
under streetlights
stopping to bolt a shot
and bet the number
of a daughter's new house—
or some other dream of his.

Wives wait
in rough-sided houses
or vaults of red brick.
They sweep the soot
from porches
and sit on swings
quietly watching
for their men climbing
the hill to them.

Their children have gone
to college or just
moved away, leaving
memory ghosts of
real towns colored dark
by the sweat of working people.

Only the night Bessemer

celebrates in a burst
of pink-orange light—
the river, the hills,
the town, the lives.

Mingo Town

"The magic thing about home is that it feels
good to leave, and it feels even better
to come back."   ~Wendy Wunder

Mingo Speaks

Listen, I'm telling you who I am, so you'll know me as yourself. There's just too much misunderstanding going around.

Mingo—from the Indians along Cross Creek, of course, and for that deeply etched face of old Chief Logan. His whole family butchered by white troops, forcing him into revenge. His story of betrayal is our own.

Junction—for all the railroad tracks crossing here, where black coal from our mines meets the red ore of barges—the red and black. To bed at night where deep dreams cross over to morning's waking to the roar and clang of the mill's making.

Steel mills rising like towers along that wide Ohio river bordering my shoulders. Nearby the bare-ass beaches and bridges where many leap crazy brave.

Yes, the land and sky and weather and surely the brick buildings facing each other along Commercial Street, smelling of beer and cigarettes; each shop with its own aroma. And yes, you people living in those houses built by families decades ago of wood and brick, nails and cement, of sweat and hope.

And all the churches where men in suits and women wearing hats enter and exit again whole. Their kids emigrating now to other cities and jobs. I've watched the young once taught in old brick buildings by educated neighbors be bussed now to hilltops and consolidated schools. I never asked for this.

I've watched you once sitting in the old theater cheering together when the cavalry arrived. Though you still cheer at touchdowns and three pointers, at concerts and school awards, most of your watching and cheering is done alone before television screens outside of the company of neighbors. The betting in backrooms has moved now to lottery tabs at store registers, yet it still speaks of dreams.

The air is cleaned now at the cost of jobs. Rogue corporations having robbed us of the dignity of making and sharing what is needed. It aches my heart. I stand with Chief Logan and cry, "Betrayal."

I ask only this: In clear morning light, wake to new hope within, share your caring as what we all need and can give, the very best of who and what we are.

Morning Comes to Mingo Town

The children carry this town
in their minds and hearts
like a prayer or poem
learned by heart, and we
nod to the gods of rivers and trees,
to cats nested on porches and dogs
running free through yards,
and to these streets and houses
so bent on surviving.

And in the playgrounds
outside of schools the
children's clear voices rise
above the sounds of mills
like a morning flock of starlings
to the ever forgiving skies.

Mingo's History Lesson

Oh, citizens, let me share with you
some history of our place.

Before these steel mills and railroads,
Before ore ovens and coal mines,
Before the drilling for oil,
Before old man Potter and his son
plotted our lots and streets for us,
Before pioneers and forts and old Washington
camping and drinking from our spring,
Before Chief Logan and the Mingo tribe
hunted and fished along our streams,
there was just this clear water and green earth,
native animals, trees, and plants.
Close your eyes and let it rise before you.
Past reaching through present.

Later, when others arrived
with splendid foreign names,
came houses and gardens,
neighborhoods and schools,
churches and stores
downtown and on corners.
The Bottoms, the Hills, all growing.
People coupled and multiplied,
mixed and spread. And I watched
and smiled unjudging, happy
to sense them renewed in the now.
Winter's dried and withered rose bush
rooted in the fertile earth
blooms again each spring.

Mother Jones Comes to Town
[From *The Autobiography of Mother Jones*]

In 1919 outside the mill gates in Mingo Junction, justice reformer and labor activist Mary Harris (Mother) Jones delivered an impassioned speech for workers and unions. It was a cool and cloudy day, and the shadows of the millworks lay across the town. These are her words:

"I was speaking in Mingo. There was a big crowd there. Most of them were foreigners, but they would stand for hours listening to the speakers, trying to fit the English words to the feelings in their hearts. Their patient faces looked up into mine. Slag, the finely powdered dust of steel mills, was ground into the furrows of their foreheads, into the lines about their mouths. The mark of steel was indelibly stamped upon them. They belonged to steel, branded as are cattle on the plains by their owners.

"I said to them, 'Steel stock has gone up. Steel profits are enormous. Steel dividends are making men rich overnight. The war—your war—has made the steel lords richer than the emperors of Rome. And their profits are not from steel alone but from your bodies with their innumerable burns; their profits are from your muscles. You go without warm winter clothes that Gary [Steel magnate Elbert H. Gary] and his gang may go to Florida and warm their blood. You puddle steel twelve hours a day! Your children play in the muck and mud puddles while the children of the Forty Thieves take their French and dancing lessons and have their fingernails manicured!'"

And the people cheered and reached up to the skies, then walked back to their homes to rest and dream.

Union Town

Once a month for decades
he brought home the Catholic Worker
folded gently and laid on kitchen table,
where it would be picked up, read,
folded, and laid back again.
A fabric in their lives,
like the Catholic prayer missals
she kept in rubber bands
folded in her dresser drawer.
He spoke little of the mill,
except of friends, left it at the mill gate
where others stop to drink away bitterness,
while he climbs the hills of home.

Their children were taught by Sisters of Charity,
Franciscans sharing Christ's caring for the poor
by having them bring cans of food each month.
At some secret signal near recess, they all
gently roll them forward on the wooden floors—
twenty cans of green beans, corn, tomato sauce…
reaching the blackboard with sweet laughter,
as the young Sister feigns surprise, then bends
to gather them up, and each and all
bow their heads in thanks.

Mingo Listens

In listening I come to know you as myself.

And I hear your cries and laughter in the days and nights. Wicked and wounded we are, tossing on the sheets, counting mill whistles till we reach over to caress the face of one we love before we rise.

Fathers and mothers, sisters and brothers rising at dawn to make a pot of oatmeal or scramble eggs as the young ones come down. Soon enough they'll be making their own.

Good neighbors mostly, we watch out and over, yet sometimes carry tales we've told ourselves. *Did you hear what Maggie did…or old Marvin…or the Smith girl or boy?* Oh, our jealous hearts, our willingness to think the worst! May we hold what's in our cup and not let it spill over onto new carpet or old ground.

There is health in our summer gardens, back yards turned over, grass traded for fresh vegetables, cared for and ripened to feed ourselves and others. Baskets of tomatoes, cucumbers, zucchini placed at neighbors' doors or taken in and shared at work.

Yes, our population has shrunken, a village once, then a town, now a village once again. We barely make the map of some government counters, yet pride ourselves on our name, yours and mine. Mingo Junction we say aloud. If they pause, we add, In the Ohio River Valley. Another long pause, and we attach ourselves to Steubenville or even up river from Wheeling. Aware that each town owns its own face and body, its own character and spirit, we yet nod.

We watch our dying mill, forced to witness much of it turned to scrap. We register how the roofs of buildings along Commercial Street have given in, fallen through, leaving gaps as from rotten teeth extracted. Yes, but we know too how others here keep the streets clean, the parks kept fresh and alive, the poor fed and cared for. And so, we smile and say, *Hey, come visit.*

At our highest point, amidst green grass and woods, the cemetery spreads out like our streets of old where neighbors rest and watch over us. And in their silence if you listen close, a sweet song of wind and trees is heard.

The Buses

for John

Steady and surely the buses run, all the way from Brilliant to Steubenville and beyond, sliding along an artery of towns every half hour. You can depend on that, unlike the infrequent cars and trains and river barges. People count on regularity getting them to work or school, uptown or down.

In morning dark, folks stand along the street awaiting the bus's soft lights of welcome where they can board the three steps, flash passes or drop their coins into the slot and take a seat.

Catholic high school girls and guys enter with clean faces yet sleepy eyes, sit and whisper their private dreams in dawning light. Women and men dressed neat in skirts and slacks are guided forward to work in shops; others in heavy work clothes head for mills and that time clock.

It's a private party, quiet like before church begins with the driver as pastor. And they steal glances at each other or look out windows at the passing buildings as familiar as their own hands and feet. They read the faces of shops opening —the drugstore, the diner, the newsstand, the bank—all in the steady pace of commerce, with bus stops and starts as smooth as food taken in and swallowed down.

When an older man dressed in neat shirt and slacks boards with a lunch pail, he and driver speak each other's names. He sits along the side by the young girl and her mother, who nods. They know him, and the mother explains, "She's going to see a doctor uptown." He smiles, the girl looks down. The mother whispers, "We had no time for breakfast." "Oh," he says then sits back and open his lunch pail. There beside the sandwich and thermos is a fine ripe banana. He takes it out and holds it toward them, an offering. The girl looks over at her mother who nods smiling, and so the fruit is passed.

Everyone watching is fed, and the driver dims the lights as the bus heads upriver.

Mingo Out Walking

Welcome to all my landscapes, its streets and corners, its yards and walkways. We still have the sidewalks that the suburbs forgot, and concrete stairs and brick alleyways for climbing our hills. When you've mounted Saint Clair or Logan Streets, McLister or Lincoln, your exercise is done, your heart clear and alive. Life is ripe here along the edge.

Walk past people out on front porches or working in their yards, their dogs barking "Hey, you!" as you pass. Three hills—North, Ravine, and Church—hold us high above our town and mill, each with its church and school buildings of old brick. No longer divided by religion, ethnic neighborhoods have melted and overflow as our bloods mix in our children.

At the foot of these hills lies Commercial Street running parallel to the river and railroad tracks stretched through the mill. Once it was home to banks and stores, drug stores and post office, bars and betting clubs, bakery and butcher shops, a white-faced Islay's rests, neighbor to an old red five & dime. Near Weisberger's Clothing stands the pool hall, a men's hostel where some overflow to steps to watch passers-by, maybe call, "Hey," and say their name aloud.

If you're up for a climb, hike all the way to Aracoma Park, where our city pool and shelter houses welcome people to drink and smoke, pitch horseshoes or roll bacci balls. Someone dares a belly whopper off the low board, others in bathing trunks and bikinis lie on towels drinking in the hot sun and music, ignoring their kids calling, "Hey, look at me."

Someone at a family picnic invites us to share meatballs or cabbage rolls, burgers or hot dogs, talking while eating and nodding to each other. Young ones search the woods for roasting sticks to burn gooey marshmallows into charcoal.

At the top of each of my hills are woods. Once entered, we escape the roar of industry and clouds of smoke. Here along the edge, life blooms. Inside nature's deep darkness we are Indians once again. We follow rough trails to where the great tire swing is cast out over the creek—daring us to belong. If you swing out far enough you can glimpse Rocky's junkyard where old cars and trucks rust into the earth.

The stones along the path accept our footfalls, and we grow silent. Sparrows and Ravens flit through trees, chipmunks and squirrels hide in the weeds, each at home where they are, and we don't need their names to know them by their presence.

At the Country Store

Outside of the town's country store
stand two girls in high school jackets,
their sports names scrawled across the back.
Laughing at the greeting of cats,
they enter, sidling their way back—
past stacks of canned goods and chips,
pastas, plates, and mugs, bottles of Coke
and maple syrup, stacks of hometown t-shirts.
Rich scent of fresh baked bread and flowers,
coffee aroma mixed with fresh cut cheese, all of it
pulling them to the meat counter.

The tall one stops, leans towards her sister,
says, "Remember now, she's just lost her son
in Afghanistan." The younger one nods,
looks up into the face of the older woman,
"Oh, Mrs, Murphy, we've come for Mom's chickens."
The older woman smiles, "Well, if it isn't Sherill...
and Marie. So good to see you girls."
Names form a sacred bond here.
"How's your sister Margaret?" Sherill asks.
"Oh, she's okay," the woman lies, not wanting
to spoil their day, like that fish someone left out.
"Well, I've got your chickens already wrapped,"
she says, eyeing their fresh faces.
At the counter she touches each girl's hand.
"You two be careful out there," she says softly
into their eyes. "You know how we need you."
A bell chimes as they exit the door.

Mingo Laments

I never asked for this.

Step onto your front porch;
breathe in smoke, kiss mill ash.
And yes, I know it means jobs
puts bread and meat on tables,
but still I hurt for the lack of
native smells of earth and trees—
maples and sycamores, fresh violets
spread along a stream.

Step into any bar in town,
smell pungent aromas
of beer and bourbon
cigar and cigarettes.
Townsfolk so good at inventing names:
The Town House, Avalon, Coochie's, Welch's,
Scaffidi's, the Argo, and Hillsboro,
Slovak and Schutzen Clubs,
Gambling above and under tables.
Yet across the street, others bargain
for cabbage and potatoes, fresh cuts of meat.

I swallow all this, good and bad eggs
feeding some desperate hunger.
I accept the rows of new houses
up on Sunrise Terrace, away from
downtown buildings falling into themselves
like drunken laborers.
Change and age unstoppable.

Yet what breaks heart and bends mind
is the ugly waste thrown in town dumps,

anti-freeze green puddles killing rats
along with violets, daisies, and trees.
The gouged and upturned earth abandoned.
The spoils of mill sewage released
into Ohio's once blue flowing waters,
the sharp stink of limp fish
dead along its shores.

Hey, I never asked for this.

MingoTown Tales

When the coal till collapsed
crushing the man and his boy,
the mines shut down,
if only for a day.
Their family name spread like a
snowstorm through town.
When the young pastor
showed up at their door
with cupcakes baked by his wife,
they turned him away.
It was too soon. It was too late.

> Stories echoed through the town again
> of the Gordon boy struck by a train
> on the old bridge, of how he must have stood
> transfixed a moment too long,
> and then was gone.

Working late at the glass plant, she crossed
the river on the railroad bridge at night,
the same tracks once where the mob had
tied down a man to threaten us all.
When she heard footsteps following
she began running madly into the dark.
When he caught her, he said, "Hey, Sue,
it's me, Rocky. Why you running?"

> In afternoon sun, the escapee abandoned his car
> and the two young captives on Main Street,
> then fled up the hill towards the woods.
> Officers Sam and Jim grabbed their guns
> in hot pursuit. Neighbors pointed them
> toward the Presbyterian church.

There on the wall he turned and stood,
then raised his gun to shoot,
and was taken down by Officer Jim,
falling into a pile of dead leaves
raked just that morning.

They lived in the company houses
in an upstairs apartment,
tobacco smoke filling the stairway.
Old man Julius, their boarder,
would sit by the window counting cars
his cigar ashtray there at his side.
Mildred would tell funny stories
a Chesterfield in her hand at all times,
a bottle of wine being passed round.
Barnie was a town fireman....
One night they stood out on the street
surrounded by neighbors, all of them
watching bright flames lick at their windows,
old man Julius, nowhere to be found.

The River

And we went down
boys and girls together
in our school clothes
along the smelly creek
all the way to the river.
Brambles and stones
beneath our feet,
we passed rails and mill gates.
And there we stood
looking out in silence
at the great river
too wide to swim across
though some might have tried
and drowned too young.
And our teacher stepped in
allowing her skirt to rise
to her hips like a cloud
with her inside, and
lifting her arms she beckoned
one by one to her side
where she blessed aloud
our baptism, not to God,
but to the waters,
and we the fish
that lived inside
and it inside of us,
"Forever and forever,"
she simply said,
"You are one."
And some laughed for joy
and some bowed their heads
and cried.

The Falls Speaks

Out the old new road, past Rocky's junkyard
overflowing with rusty cars and barking dogs,
'round the bend at Ottie's chicken farm, then
across the old stone bridge, there's that grassy field
and a path that winds along a small stream
to our falls at old Cross Creek.

And you journey here in couples or groups,
intent on wading out into my waters,
risking rapids, you step on slippery rocks
like Jesus on the waters. And the sun
warms you enough so you slip off shirts and blouses,
roll up trousers or lift skirts up the thigh.
Together you laugh and call out, at last immersed
in earth's sweet baptism.

Mingo Dreams

It's hard to be a city at night, sleeping along this big river. So much wakes you from slumber—mill whistles, sirens, dogs barking, people falling up and down stairs, babies crying to be fed or changed, couples making loud love in bedrooms or cars. When it comes down to it, I wake even when doors slam and when people shout too loud and long.

Oh, I still watch over you—mother-father to a tribe awake or asleep. And yes, I worry about floods and fires, heart attacks, and auto accidents. I'm also there for all births and deaths. I count you all as precious, though I do accept nature's course—Flow like a river, open like a sky./ Feed the heart, yet bow the head.

Sometimes in night's quiet middle, I dream of fish flying about the room, trains climbing up my back and arms, skirts twirling at my face, golden hair falling over milky breasts— Yes, I'm alive! And sometimes nightmare phantoms swirl in mill light, then creep along streets to peep into windows, carrying guns and knives.

In one dream, our mill rolls up like a newspaper then drifts away downriver. We all stand mute like at the end of a long game. As it fades to darkness, I jerk myself awake, then lie there 'till breathing softens and I reach over again to turn on the streetlights.

I rise to the rich smell of coffee being brewed in houses, the sounds of people showering, dressing for work, getting kids off to schools, maybe saying a few silent prayers for self and others. All of us meeting the day, all of us working through our dreams.

The Mingo Show

Fourteen cents was the ticket price for years at the Mingo Show, till they finally upped it to a dime and a nickel. So, we took back pop bottles, ran errands for neighbors, and went to the movies often. On Friday and Saturday *High Noon* might be showing, and on Sunday, Monday, and Tuesday *The Quiet Man* would play. In the middle of the week, on Wednesday and Thursday, you could catch a showing of *A Streetcar Named Desire*. The lives on the screen extended our own as we stretched into the fresh anguish of Marlon Brando or James Dean, as we packed it in at the OK Corral with Burt Lancaster and Kirk Douglas. For working-class kids, we traveled much in our own hometowns. The theater was our watering hole for the imagination of what could be.

Sometimes, if I had done my homework and if Grandma was going, so that Mom had no sitter, I could go along for the midweek showing of a film like *Born Yesterday*. It would be dish and bingo night, and the lights would be on as the usher (a friend's older brother, or a kid who had graduated from his paper route) would hand us our gravy boat which Mom and Grandma would cradle on their laps beside me.

On bingo night after the first showing, the lights would come on. We could all suddenly see each other. The place would be packed with smiling neighbors and kids rubbing the sleep from their eyes. "Mingo Mike" Kendrach, the manager, would come out onto the stage with a couple of grinning ushers rolling in the bingo board and balls. He would tap the microphone a couple times and ask, "Is this on?" To which we would all shout back, "No, it's on!" and roar with laughter. Then he would smile and declare, "Good evening, everyone. And welcome to the Mingo Show." It seems now that the general response to this was a kind of relieved laughter.

Then Mike would get serious as he announced, "Tonight, ladies and gentlemen, there will be fifty numbers called in our game. And I remind you that tonight's grand prize is..." (There was silence here, just to be certain we knew the stakes.) "... 200 dollars!" Real sighs went up at the sound of the amount, for most of we kids had already spent it in our heads buying new bikes, our parents, new refrigerators. "Yes, 200 dollars is tonight's prize," Mingo Mike would declare, and I could watch my mom holding her card as she smiled down on me, as if to say, "Boy, wouldn't your father be surprised."

Once, when my brother was off in college, I watched as his best friend won the coverall jackpot for $100 and $50 worth of merchant coupons—a free haircut at Toni's, shoe repair at Arman's, a large sundae at Islay's, a $10 tool at Gilchrest Lumber, and pool game at Dugan's. As fate had arranged, it was the night before he shipped out in the Navy, so he never got to collect.

Mingo Mike would begin by reminding us to take the free space on our card (only those who payed adult prices received cards), and he would begin the reading of the balls handed to him by the smiling usher from a guest ball-drawer. About 10 balls in he would caution us, "Remember, this is a cover-all game. All spaces must be covered in order to win." But we were still young and into the game, and those odds seemed about right. Later, when he announced, "Ladies and gentlemen, we have only five numbers left," you could hear a bridge of sighs stretch across the audience—a sympathetic acceptance of our mutual fate.

Usually there were no grand winners, but always we each had won. We had shared the common experience of America—in the film and in each other. I carry lots of those old films within me for their human themes and gestures. I also still carry the warm faces of the people I lived with—my neighbors and friends, even my enemies and their moms, the folks from North Hill, Reservoir Hill, Church Hill, and the Bottom: the old women behind us who chattered in strange tongues— Slovak, Italian, Polish, Hungarian—their dark-eyed daughters sitting with their mustached beaus, my black friends nested in the back corner, my English teacher and her best friend.

Whether in a melting pot or rich salad bowl of American life, the experience made us all human and together. And as we piled out of the theatre into the evening light, people smiled into each other's eyes as they joked about losing the grand prize—"And what would I do if I won—buy a new mink coat!" There was good cheer to spare. And as we walked out into the night, I would take the soft hands of my mother and grandmother, and together we would climb the streets of home.

First Dance

Yes, the boys sit or stand
along the gymnasium wall,
while the girls flit along the edge.
Unlike their days of holding hands
and marching round the gym,
their eyes glance up and down
while the music plays, and
in skirts or slacks,
their hips begin to sway,
.

And then the Principal appears
without his suit and tie
to call them out into the middle.
and speak the words they long for:
"Now choose a partner…everyone."

The eyes go up, the hands go out,
the breath quickens with the heart.
To touch this other, to smell their hair,
to glide together, bodies linked,
is the softness inside a dream,
and there they float.

But then the music stops—
"Okay now," is called,
"you must choose a different partner."
And so another rite begins.

Paddy's Diner

Don't tell me it's just about the cooking,
and swallow that "greasy spoon" talk.
It's a diner, for Pete's sake.
Everybody knows that.

You go there for the breakfast special
bacon and eggs with a stack and toast,
all served with coffee and conversation,
by a waitress who calls you Sweetie and Hon.
The crowd changes, maybe neighbors,
maybe people you went to high school with.
If there's time, Joe, the owner-cook,
comes out to ask how's everything
and how're your brother or sister getting along.

Okay, the dinners aren't the best,
except for Joe's fish on Fridays,
and Marie's meatloaf on Sundays,
and Bertha serving beef tips
and noodles—anytime.
You learn what to ask for,
and you always leave a tip,
in bills and no small change.

Late at night folks out drinking
show up for a steaming plate
of French fries and gravy, sparked
with hot sauce or ketchup.

Marie's mother makes those pies
and those glazed Sunday donuts.
Call it what you want. I know
railroaders and truckers name it
a little piece of heaven.

Rocky's Junkyard

Otto's farm grows junked cars
dead seeds in the mud.
Three cinder-block buildings
handle the trade
while the dark entrails of engines
hang from pulley chains.

Tires, radiators, axels
stacked to the roofs.
Salvage they call it now.

Inside the main building
a barrel stove warms Rocky's wife
who takes calls and works the books.
Rocky just grins and grabs his gloves
moves steady into the cold.
Day and night now the cars
burn in winter light.

Steel Mill Track-Gang

Work begins round the clock
when your shift begins and you're
at your station or the foreman
sends you out with your crew.
Gloves and shovel in hand,
hard hat and steel toes
guarding you, you head out
down the steel or slag alleys
hot sparks seeking your skin.
The weather eats at your face
and hands. Blast furnace heat
sweats through your shirt.

When you get there, you pick up
what others have put down:
clearing track, opening sewers,
carrying lime sacks, punching pig iron
out from their molds, swallowing
dirt and body pain.
All we workers making things real
over and over again…till you
begin thinking of your lunch pail,
of laughter back in the locker-room.

Inside the steady roar, you
speak with your hands—
thumb up for when work is done,
but the work is never done; it's 24/7
till one day…the mill closes down
and you return to your homes
maybe talk to your wife, walk
the kids to school, sit around
on porches watching, listening,

enduring the life of the
workless man or woman.

Finally, you go downtown to
the bars outside the mill gate,
where you nod to the others
all of you waiting, waiting, waiting
to be let back in.

Wages

Payday comes in from the cold
and sets a bag down in the hallway.
She finds her place at the table
where we are dressed in our good clothes.
Mom is already drinking wine
and Dad is telling funny work stories.
Payday laughs like coins falling on a metal tray.
We pass her the pork chops
and watch her fork not one but two—
"One for later," she grins at us.
Like always we pretend to smile.

By the time the sun has set
we've said good-bye to our Payday
and a silence fills the room.
When I break a plate, Mom cries,
"Oh shit. Look what you've done."
You can hear the sound of wind.
Then Mom hands Dad a fist full of bills,
and we kids go off to our rooms.
Tomorrow will mean our old clothes again
and the counting of our coins.

These Church Steps

Along the great building standing like a brick ship
are these church steps where so many photos were taken:
for 90 years a succession of Catholic girls and boys
standing tall, while staring back at the camera,
and those choirs and bands and clubs each special
if only for the moment—Click.

How many wedding parties—parents and neighbors
there beside brides and grooms smiling in
innocence about to be shed in bright sunlight.
A button clicks, a car passes, and it's gone,
love to last an eternity through change.

At the back of the church, beneath the sanctuary
the stairs take you down into rich aromas
of beef and ham, pastas bathed in tomato sauce.
Strong women in aproned armor are feeding all
through passage rites upstairs—from baptism to death,
bingo here are Friday nights...

Beside the church, the good Sisters' house
where young and old, they eat and laugh,
sing and pray at night and each morning
pray again before the town's children,
teaching and demanding respect for God
and caring for each other.

In the rectory house nearby a succession of priests
and their housekeepers make a quiet life.
As ship's captain surrounded by white-clad youth
he appears at the altar to bless and transform.
Then again, for all photos as a stamp of validation
he arrives on these steps for this and for the going
out into the world.

Marching Band

Standing beneath stadium lights,
I breathe onto my fingers
warming them to work the cornet's valves.
Across the field the rows of crowds
huddle against the wind.
"This is crazy," Janey says,
"Yeah," I say, "and we're doing it."

A whistle calls and six majorettes
drop blankets from bare legs.
If they can stand it, so can we.
Our lines straighten, instruments rise,
again, we blow our air to warm them.
"Right guard," someone calls.
A drumroll beats, and we march
out under bright lights.
Behind us a train whistle hoots,
the steel mill roars, and the director
calls, "Play your best," We answer back
with our notes from Sousa.
All numbness and cold spent now on the crowd
which greets our sacrifice with sweet applause.

Running in the 1960s

At three each spring day
they come running
in gray cotton sweat suits
heading out of town.
Young boys training for track
breathing hard, finding pace
inside cool April winds,
green everywhere around them.

In weeks they will round the track
under stadium lights, leaping
and dashing, hurdling, and holding out
in the long runs, some passing batons
linking efforts of others, hurting
at doing their level best.

Their sisters are at home
doing schoolwork, helping Mom
with dishes and sorting things.
And one out watching young siblings
play in the yard chases their frisbee
passing the boys, who for a moment,
note her swift legs and arms, her hair
streaming in the wind, yet keep
running on.

Sweet Dreams

During the night, Joyce appears to me as in an old school photo of us together. Her face pale eyes blue as ever. "You must go to my old house," she whispers slowly. "There's someone there you need to meet…"

I nod my head and somehow I am there at her back door. The house is nearly empty and so I enter without knocking. I pass through the kitchen with its old smells of food and cigarettes and down a hallway.

In the sunny living room, I see a young girl about 12 (age of my granddaughter) sitting on a hammock in a blue dress. She looks up to me with a clear smiling face, so innocent yet familiar.

There is this long pause where we can hear each other breathing. Then she whispers, "I'm the child of your friendship." My heart wakens and I reach out to her with both arms and hands…she reaches up to me.

"The child of our friendship," I say to myself and her. I take her hands, and I awaken.

Again and again, I try to go back, but cannot.

Brothers

Hey, Bob, can you come in and cover for me? I gotta go see Jen. It's kind of an emergency…

…Someone sick or dying?

No.

…Well, then, no, man, I got some things going right now.

If you gotta know, Jen's pregnant. She just did 3 p-tests and won all three. Blues lined up and down…Blue, Blue, Blue…I know, I'm only laughing 'cause I'm so damn lost and don't know what to do next.

…"Shit or go blind," Pop used to say. "Ass or a hole in the ground," kind of thing….Is it…?

Sure it's mine. What you think! Christ man, I'm no dope and Jen is no whore.

…Let me think a minute, Tom.

Well, if you can just cover for me, I'll do your night shifts next week. Man, I just gotta be with her right now, I know that much.

Pause…

…Okay, I gotta drop the kids off at Marie's mom's place. But I'll get there soon as I can.

Hey, Bob, you know this means a lot to me, Bro. And, hey, don't tell Mom or Sis or nobody, really, till Jen and I work this all out. Hell, I guess I'm caught between that rock and a hard place, and we'll turn it over and see if I'm a snake or a father.

…Yeah, well, listen, Bro, I'm pulling for you, and always have.

Sisters

"Hey, Barb, Margaret's at the emergency room....
....
No, the EMT squad came and got her again.
....
They didn't say nothing—couldn't really,
not doctors, you know....
....
Yeah, it's her heart I think. But still,
wearing an oxygen mask, she waved
up at me from her cart....
....
Me, I'm going to work as usual.
Someone got to open the shop, and
we've got half a dozen orders to fill,
all those cold cuts to chop....
....
Of course, I love her, she's our sister,
for Christ's sake, but you know
she'd want me to open....
....
70 years and we never closed shop
'cept holidays and when Mom and Pop died."

Silence...

"Listen, you keep me in touch, hear.
I love you and I'll see you when I can."

Letters

She wrote him from across the ocean, the older sister of his bunkmate, Al. "I live here with my mom and pop on the shores of Lake Cumberland, and I work at the church cleaning and typing up. I am pleased to write you and be friends. Do write back. Sincerely, Sherill."

All day while digging trenches, he thought of this invitation—a woman back home writing to me in the Philippines. He was fighting the war with a blade and shovel, clearing the forest for the planes to land. The days were long like the war. Yes, he would write her back home and learn about women.

"Greetings, Miss Sherill, I desire to write to you and would be pleased to be your pen pal. Your brother Al showed me your pretty photo and thought we might become friends. I do hope so. It is hot here and there are all kinds of strange birds and trees. We've seen no Japanese, yet we stand ready, though I don't know for what. How is life in Kentucky? Your would-be friend, Harry."

Once a week their letters pass like carrier pigeons over land and water, and so they grew to know and like each other well. His days and nights now had some purpose, to visit Sherill when the war was over and done. He felt himself grow more friendly with others, trusting himself more. From nature he learned the names and ways of animals and plants, and shared them with her.

She wrote of her seven brothers and how they all worked on tobacco farms, how they hoed and harvested, then cured it in big barns. "You gotta come see it, Harry, when this big war is done. Yours, Sherill Ann." Sharing her middle name was to him like holding hands, and he told her so. A romance of words on paper was growing like her tobacco or his tomato garden back home in Ohio.

In early August of 1945 the bombs were dropped on Japan, so that when his father died days later, Harry was not allowed leave to return home. Yet he knew that soon he would be returning home where he could be himself with Sherill. Things had moved so far along that a proposal was offered. "Sweet Sherill Ann, I have come to love you and want you in my life always. I will be with you soon."

He wanted for the war to end and needed to hear her response, but suddenly he was told to pack up, they would be shipping home.

Back in Ohio, he kissed his mother, shook the hand of his brother who told him the railroad was hiring. Then, on a windy September day, he stood by his father's grave to whisper hello and tell of his new life with Sherill. He had put his military clothes away in the chest the army had given him. He bought good civilian clothes, including a fine suit and a pair of shiny black dress shoes. As soon as he heard from her, he would drive his father's Dodge south to Kentucky, where he would meet Sherill and her family, and where he and Sherill would marry.

===

Now, reader, here is where you create your own ending. Experience may dictate to you from what life lessons you have learned, or your imagination and heart can guide you here.

Some may see Sherill and Harry happily married with a couple kids, he working on the mill's railroad and growing a garden, she singing in the choir, working as secretary in the church, and caring for his mom.

Others may see those shoes which he kept in a box under his bed, and know they never saw the light of day. For, one night, Harry burns them in the coal furnace as he stands looking on. Next morning, as usual, Harry eats the breakfast his mother makes for him, then carries his lunch box off to work in the mill and never speaks of those shoes again.

The choice is yours.

The Coach

"Honey, when you go downtown, could you pick up some things from the market?"

"Oh, hey, I'm not going down today."

"Yeah, how come? You always go down on Saturday mornings."

"Hmmp."

"What's goin' on, hon?"

"Well, were you at the gym for the game last night or not?"

"Oh, hon, that loss wasn't your fault. Don't take it all on. It's the team that lost."

"50 to 88, Clare, that's not a loss, it's a disaster. Like this here burnt toast, it ain't easy to swallow down."

"Oh, don't do this to yourself."

"Well, you know those guys downtown outside the pool hall will do it to me. They'll spit it right in my face. I mean 2 wins and 8 losses ain't easy to defend."

"Yeah, and I'm sure not going to say, 'It's just a game,' again. I know how long you've worked to be head coach serving as assistant through two head coaches. I know it hurts, babe."

"Oh, Clare, I'm a failure to the boys, the school, and this town. If I lose this badly this season, I'll be let go as coach and…as teacher, and then I'll be a failure to you and myself."

* * *

"You still sitting there? Well, here's the paper. You can read about the war in Syria, the virus spreading the world, or look closer to home where a fire burned a house down on Clifton Avenue last night."

"You know, I was just sitting here remembering old coach Walker, and what he said one game when we was losing terrible. He was taking lots of pressure then too. So what he said that night was for him and us, 'Listen, men, all you can do here is be the best at who you are.'"

"That's really good."

"Yeah it is. You know, I got to go see if one of my boys lived near that fire. Hey, what was it you needed from the market..."

Why I Read Books

I am home from college
resting on our back porch
in a webbed lawn chair
when Dad comes through
on his way to the garage.
I look up from my book,
Anderson's *Winesburg, Ohio*,
and he stops, takes a breath,
then asks it, "Son, do you ever think
of doing something...instead
of just reading a book?"
I am struck, hard swallow,
and shrug a simple smile.
Dad is a railroader
always finding work, and I
his pathetic son right now,
waiting to find a summer job.

He disappears down the steps
but returns five minutes later
for something he's forgotten.
Ready now, I enter the house,
"Wait, Dad, can I speak?"
He turns from the sink.
"Yeah, what's up, boy?" I am
20, yet glad to be his 'boy.'
"Dad, I want to answer you."
He nods, and facing each other, I try,
"I don't know if I can say it right,
but some of these books...
well, they have honestly saved me...
and kept me going."

We stand in that great quiet,
two men sharing a felt connection
like a prayer offered
and accepted.
We are not the hugging Smiths
yet we both feel held.

Hometown Immigrant—2020

While my wife sits with her aunt
in the hospital room, I drive around town,
familiar yet changed in ways I don't understand.
Downtown is full of emptiness,
buildings leaning hard on each other
like old men in a food line, and I
try to smile and accept all this,
yet search for a neighbor's eyes,
someone to know my name.

I've become an immigrant here.

Old church buildings fold over like cardboard.
The Presbyterian where we trudged
Sunday mornings in stiff shirts and dresses
is all boarded and shuttered,
yet I stop and get out, climb the steps,
and cross the door's broken glass.
For a moment, I close my eyes
and see again the forms of others
sitting close inside the roar
of organ and choir echoing.
Sudden comes the Bam! of a person
or animal running wild inside,
and I choose to back away,
get back in car and drive
up these hills of change.

What I write of this place
lives on in memory now,
like an old love affair or divorce.
And I have come all this way to find home
yet struggle to embrace.

Working Wisdom

Dawn opens the day; dusk puts it to sleep.
Sunlight spreads; night darkness enfolds.
And in between we work and rest, think and feel,
care for each other, brother and sister, father and mother,
neighbors and friends, and those in need or giving care.

Our saints wear levy and broadcloth, shirts and slacks;
we glove our hands when needed, wear coats out in the cold.
Grandmas wear house dresses, maybe scarves; grandfathers
make wine in cellars, garden the foot of the yard.
We get by without needing fame,
seek self instead, up close where wholeness thrives.

The streets of this town blend far and near.
To have just what we need is wisdom, and we
work shifts for it in factories and hospitals,
making the ordinay sacred by caring.
No rewards, doing what's to be done.
There are doors we need to pass through.

Our eating bowl contains the world;
our candles melt ignorance and hate.
"World without end," we say, bower
and bowed to the same,
seeing ourselves as One.
Wind chimes hang in space,
turning empty wind to music.

Early Memories

Love begins by taking care of the closest ones—
the ones at home. ~Mother Teresa

Along the Ohio

Frost rises along the tracks,
white feathered branches in the light.

Blue barges of coal
work their way upriver
past houses sleeping late
through Sunday morning.

Backyard sparrows
line the wooded fences
without any necks
waiting for breadcrumbs.

Thin plumes of chimney smoke
rise straight to the sky.

Our House on Murdock Street

Our house was never
more than that. Our yard
was not a lawn. We cut
the grass with a push mower
every two weeks.
We painted the eaves when they
blistered and flaked.
In winter
we hauled our ashes
out to the alley. We swept
the porch each week.

        Inside
things were kept casual
but clean. At night
the counter would be
cleared, our shoes thrown
into the closet, our beds
made the way we'd left them.

And yet we got by
taking what we had
to pay the bills
for four kids.
Dad worked two jobs—
railroad and furnaces.
Mom cared for us, kept
food on the table, read us
books at bedtime,
that's how
we got by.

        And this…

When our friends
came over, Mom would
feed us, listen to
our stories, laugh and
dance along to our music.

I remember
the first week
of my father's
two-week vacation,
he spent planting saplings
along the highway
across the street.

What more does it take?

What Is Near

I pass my mother aproned at the stove
who turns to wave a wooden spoon
fresh from the cabbage soup, and I go
down into the basement smell where
father stands at his sound-cutting lathe.

We nod, do not speak, await
what is to come—the wood's shape.

At the workbench I search the wooden drawers
for bolts and nuts that fit. I tighten the vice,
spin the wing nut down its shank, nothing more
than this in the whir of spinning wood.

This is the standing by of us—
this is the finding of our way.

Thieves

Four young boys enter the old Five and Dime store on Main Street, their sole intention to shoplift something—anything—a mechanical pencil, a pocket tablet, a hair comb, a pair of cleats for shoes. They try not to laugh as they look around at each other. The one boy is keeping the clerk busy with questions, while the others slip stolen goods into jeans' pockets, then slide out the side door.

Out on the street down by the Isaly's store, their laughter is released, and they share their booty in broad sunlight. They have proven themselves to each other and do not notice the man standing along the wall. In a sharp moment he steps forward grabbing one boy by the arm, losing hold of another as they run down the street. All are breathing hard, but none as much as the captive. He looks up into the man's angry face and receives the answer. "I'm the owner of that store, you damn little thief."

The boy tries to apologize, but the man's anger eraser all defense. "You're going to pay for this. All of you thieves will be examples to others in this goddamn town." He holds out his hand, and the boy places the tiny metal cleats there, muttering, "I'll pay you for this." But the man is already pulling him along toward the policeman standing outside of the drug store.

In a few minutes the boy will give up all the names. The officer will say, "I know this boy's father." He knows all of their families. It's a small town, and already the boy tastes shame.

Once released, he rushes up the hill towards home. He must first warn his friends, and then tell his father.

II.

"Why would you do such a thing? You've been brought up better than that. Now haven't you?" Her words pierce like knife wounds, and yet he knows her forgiveness will follow after a day or two. He is still her son no matter what he's done. There is still a "we" to cover all.

His father is another thing, and, sitting in the front room wordlessly waiting for him is punishment already begun. His little sister passes, shaking her head.

Finally, a car engine pulls up, the front door opens, and his mother rushes to meet him in the hallway. "Let me fill you in on what your boy has done," she says, and the boy tries to hear his charges. "He was caught stealing at the Five and Dime downtown an hour ago. The police called me."

Pause, a question, then answer: "Oh, a dumb pair of shoe cleats. That doesn't matter. What matters is the new owner wants to press charges against him and the three hooligans he hangs with. The mayor's going to hold a hearing at 4:00 today."

Pause again. The father enters the room shaking his head, ambushed by his own family here. He looks into the boy and asks, "Okay now, what's the story, boy?"

"Guilty as charged," the boy quips nervously.

"Don't you make light of this," comes with a stare. "You're in some deep trouble, boy. Now, stand up!"

He is three quarters his father's size, and his head is bowed now as he swallows his broken heart. "I'm sorry," comes from his mouth. He can read the deep pain in his father's eyes, who makes no attempts to strike him.

"You've hurt this family deeply, son. You've damaged us all." All air is drained from the room.

The boy now sees himself as a rag on the floor. He wants to step on it, kick it aside, then throw it into the trash. He says softly, "Please, Dad, may I go up to my room now, where I belong?"

Milltown, Ohio

Where waiting for my physical to begin summer work
I overhear the mill doctor tell a man
he has black lung and will be dying soon.

Where people who dream numbers on Monday to Saturday
bet 50 cents-a-day (boxed), and on Sunday
drop $3 in the church baskets.

Where under the stadium lights of April
sons run their hearts out or clash in October
gaining ground with their taut armored bodies

Where fathers labor in boredom and sweat
for love of their children, yet sit in Rose's Café
where no one can touch them.

Where majorette daughters march to the altar
splitting their lives forever between working
and being a mother in love.

Where mothers serve cabbage rolls and cornbread or
spaghetti and salad, or bean soup with ham
and wonder at 50 where their life has cooked away to.

Where Jack O'Reedy
30 years a roomer at Grandma Ferroni's
50 years a pipe-fitter in the mills
sits by night at his window gazing out
past the town, the mill, the river, to
count the busses to Wheeling.

Of such a life
        lived for and despite itself
let no one judge.

My Working-Class Education

FIRST

In first grade we lined up for everything. Saying the alphabet helped us know our place. I came near the end. I knew that, though I didn't know why. What was order to a kid of five? My memory was a seed garden growing each day as I fed it snacks of graham crackers and milk. There was my Roy Rogers pencil box that I forgot at school that first day, and someone kept it with its sliding drawer and the good smell of erasers.

We lined up for everything, like I said—music and gym, lunch and recess, getting our coats on to go home. And one time we stood along the steps at the nurse's office to stand at her lap as she ran a piece of dry spaghetti through our hair. We just didn't ask.

SECOND

Mrs. Reisling spoke to us soft. She was small but we listened to each word—like spiders dancing over water, coins pressed into our hands. She smelled of flowers in rain when she touched us with our names.

I remember one day seeing myself in the window as I stood at the back sharpening my pencil. She was watching me. I was someone too. I would do good work, lay things out straight, clean up after myself without asking.

THIRD

My third grade teacher, Mrs. Brettel, was my mother's friend, but I was not her child. She was the one who taught me to love birds, feeding us drawings of them to color each Thursday after gym. These were the birds I watched around our yard each morning and night. And I would rub and rub those crayons into each bird's pale skin till it felt warm and sticky like blood.

I remember how we couldn't believe Mrs. Brettel had a son and a daughter, even though she talked of them. We thought they were storybook kids. Then one day she brought the boy to class because he was too sick to go to school and too young to stay home alone. He sat at my desk with me, a quiet brother.

FOURTH

She held my hand as we marched around the gym floor, and her hand wasn't cold or wet like the others, but warm in a way that made me sing inside. Her dress brushed my fingers and I felt myself turn like a bird flying through the sun.

When she moved away, I vanished too. I was a fish without air, a poem without words.

FIFTH

I was taken in by the twins. After all, there were two of them, and they danced together for my birthday party. "First you put your two knees/ close up tight..." Only there were four knees, not two, doubling my delight as they tapped and shuffled, kicked and turned on our linoleum floor. "Could-she love, could-she woo, could-she, could-she, could-she coo!" It was years before I knew those were words and not just sounds of a flirting girl.

My mother baked a huge cake, in the shape of a fire truck, but we fed all the kids cupcakes with thick sugared icing.

SIXTH

Shirley said I was too young to kiss her that way. I'd seen it in a movie once. This was a game we were playing at a birthday party, going into the other room alone together.

Outside I could hear the trains, and I stood near her holding hands in the dark light of the window. I put my hand in the small of her back as she leaned into my face. Her lips were smooth as rain.

SEVENTH

We threw the basketball so long our arms grew warm. Then we ran rings around the point dribbling till we passed, pivoting into the nest. We loved the ball loving us. Five of us on a side, the coach commanding all of us to share the ball, drive into the net, get back on defense. It made such sense. We gave our lives to it.

EIGHTH

On the blackboard the teacher wrote the names. Honor Role it said, and I was never up there, never one of the chalked ones, due to be erased in six weeks. I was busy studying the way girls' necks looked in the window light as they reached up to pull the blinds, the soft sway of skirts up the aisle, the warm smell of lilacs, the thin hair on their arms, the transparence of skin across their wrists.

I studied enough to get by, not too much to become unpopular. My locker held my books at night as I burst out the door—eager to drop my innocence, holding strong to my ignorance.

NINTH

I fell in love with unreality in the semi-dark of the movie house, then on the steps before school—where the girls stood before the brick, like sibyls and sirens mesmerizing my heart.

And so, I bought an old guitar with my newspaper money, wore my fingertips to callouses over bone, sliding them up and down the long neck till the chords cried out and fell like rain over the town. It was my own blood pulse I heard behind the notes climbing into space then falling over everything. And I raced through records following the sound down streets, running it back through strings and wood, vibrating it through my legs and arms, biting off notes, releasing others, pounding the strings like drums, over my own little town.

TENTH

I loved reading as a kid; then like an oaf, I'd misplaced it for running the streets and rock and roll music. I found it again in book report choices... *Huck Finn* by Mark Twain, *Main Street* by Sinclair Lewis, *Winesburg, Ohio* by Sherwood Anderson—I didn't know there could be books like these.

So in my head whole worlds began to breathe. I'd watch people at the stadium, in the theater, on the buses, and their lives would cross over into mine. When they got off, I'd continue with them up the hill and into the houses of their lives.

I began to write it down. It was like learning to dance for the first time or watching a film at a drive-in where the movie plays while the lives go on inside each car, and all you had to do was listen close inside yourself.

I didn't tell this to anyone.

ELEVENTH

The coal truck backed over the curb and into our house. He said he was turning his rig around to unload. Mother cried at the cracked plaster and glass all over the living room rug, and father hadn't even been told yet.

I knew this would make the papers that night, "Truck Backs Into House." We lived in a small town. Soon it would all be cleaned up and fixed, but forever people would speak of it, the house with the truck in it.

At school the next day I was a hero or something, and for what? I wasn't even there when the back gate came loose and dumped a load of coal into the yard. But I did help shovel it into the face of the coal shoot for hours when Dad came home and made the deal—the coal was free, and $100 for the broken house. That was the short of it.

The long of it was my mother's fear of leaving the house alone again. Someone always had to be home to welcome such things.

TWELFTH

We were playing euchre down in Ken's family room. The record player was chanting, "Take a Message to Mary" and in the chorus, we all looked up to sing. "Take a message to Mary.../ but don't tell her where I am."

I was in love with Barbara then, fair faced and pony-tailed, with a brain that ran like a train. She helped me with my civics and biology; I helped her with math and English. We stood at each other's locker before and after school.

When Barbara told me she was going to college someday, it sounded like a place to visit. I had a brother off at college in Tennessee then. But what does that mean—college? Where I asked? She didn't answer, but looked up slowly from her book with sad eyes asking, What about you? What will you do with yourself after you graduate? I saw two roads before me: one down the hill and into the mills, and the other out the highway and on to college.

That night as I watched my friends laying down their cards one by one in silence, I started adding up the points. And I asked myself, What will I do with myself? Slowly I began counting backwards all the way to one.

Reunion at Cross Creek

Walking down the hills of home
to the near side of the river,
a light snow in morning sun.

Back at the house, people rising
taking hot showers, combing hair,
eggs turned to suns on plates.

I have gone out to a place
where we once fished along a creek:
the whisper of traffic overhead
on the bridge near the tracks.
A dozen starlings root among leaves
on the frozen bank.

I close my eyes over forty years
and my brother appears on the other side
bending to light us a fire.
Let's see what's biting here, he says,
We'll go home in a little while.

I sit on a log counting breaths, slowly
disappearing in the snowy dawn.

Delivering Papers

I used to take papers in this town,
the morning route passed on by my brother,
Pittsburgh Post Gazette and *Wheeling Intelligencer*
rolled and dropped on porches in the dark,
to be opened in morning light and read before
work or after getting the kids off to school.

I would roll as I walked keeping it tight
and twisting it up over the top, then
dropping it back in the canvas bag
hung over my shoulder.
Up the hill I would climb
keeping an eye out for dogs,
watching window lights come on. Once
a pretty girl in night gown smiled down
as I gazed back, then moved along.

My best customers were not on the books.
Big Tony would send me back to Bessy's
for a sandwich of ham and cheese,
then pay me a quarter, a tenth of my pay.
And up on Madison, old Mr. Henry
would be waiting in his garden to
buy my "extra" then ask how I was doing
and show me what was growing.
Before I quit the route to work at the dinner,
his wife had died, and someone said he'd
shot his dog and become a hermit. By then I could
almost understand the news, but not such grief.

For a time, I'd sneak a smoke at the hilltop,
and once I had to poop in the woods.
Though the work had become a part of me,

I asked my folks why people get the paper.
Dad laughed and said they read
to get the "number" from the day before.
Mom said she knows on Mondays
they read to see who died and survived.
I shook my head but knew somehow
my work had purpose. The town crier,
when I turned at the hilltop to walk home,
I would survey the town as dawning light
spread along the streets, on houses and trees,
down to the mill's steaming cauldrons and rails,
and I would know somehow, I owned this town, and
what's more, this town owned me.

Out the Old "New Road"

At the bridge beyond the dogs
people swim in a yellowed creek.
In cut-off jeans and t-shirts
they wade out beyond the mud.
People—like we were once—
standing there amidst the weeds.

I peel a thorny milkweed pod,
touch the white blood,
release the birds inside.

There was a gray house here,
chickens clucking in the yard.
Across the road a cow trough
all glazed with green moss
near the old spring house.

Once while we drank here
my friend's older brother
told how his mother
lifted their old fallen Ford
from his aching chest.

Rock and Rolling in the Early 1960s

"Don't forget where you came from."
~A working-class oath.

We were two high school rock groups
briefly merged into one in our
small mill town.

The Vibrations and the Fidels—
our names spelled out the dream.
The Vibrations grew out of band camp
jamming in the men's barracks,
playing while whirling majorettes
danced before the bonfire.
Joey, Rich, Bill, and I.

The Fidels had crooned doo-wop
in locker room showers, bounced
their sound off restroom tiled walls.
Noony, Donny, Nick, Guy, John, and Pete.

After a month of practicing
in family basements and garages,
we were ready for our first gig.
So we worked extra hours
as ushers and fry cooks,
or borrowed money from our families
to buy the matching shirts—
maroon long sleeves—
at Weisberger's Clothing downtown.

Our big gig was a sock hop
at the "Wigwam" Community Center.
We came early to set up:
two amps, two mics,

three guitars, and a set of drums.
We were our own roadies;
someday we might have groupies.
Out in the back alley
we smoked our last cigarettes.
Police cruisers gleamed in the parking lot,
kids played under streetlights a block away
as the mills roared and the night Bessemer
spread its scrim of orange-pink light.

At ten after the hour, we were introduced,
and so, strolled out from the back room
in our new shirts, to a shower of hometown applause.
Friends and enemies gathered
to measure our sound.

And we had it that night—
playing our eight songs
from somewhere deep inside,
without really trying, in that
easy effort of riding a wave.
Our intention lay in each note,
each beat, each chord change.
It echoed off the walls, and
sunk into the dancing bodies.

Doo-wop and rock and roll,
rockabilly and rhythm and blues,
we played it all, lifting ourselves
and our town above the noise and dirt.
It rocked and rolled right out of us.
We were part of that dream.
We were bringing it home.
We were making it real.

Things My Father Taught Me

Wakened by his footsteps
as he dressed in morning dark,
I'd lie there awaiting his
call to rise and shine.
He moved with purpose
like the railroad. His hands
wore the callouses of work;
his eyes were dark pools of trust.
He taught with what he was,
with words like apples
sweet and tart—

    Trust the road
    that takes you.
        Let the saw
        do its work.
    The worst fear
    is fear of work.
        Let the shovel
        throw the dirt.
    Enjoy the work you do
    and the job will answer back.
        Let the hammer
        drive the nail.

Drawn down into his basement
where our hair was cut,
my brother and I sat
'round his heavy workbench
awaiting his words of manhood.
We grinned to see him blush,
look away to drills and saws.
Yet he spoke simply from his life—

Women are there
to be cared for.
Love them as yourself.
    The wrong you make
    goes on until you claim it.
Family blood extends
to everyone.
    When you speak ill of another
    you speak ill of yourself.

And from the father who
never struck me, who
seldom touched me,
whose knuckles were Boy Scout knots,
whose muscled arms were tools—

    When you begin to lie
    you start to sell yourself.
        Don't confuse your wants
        with your needs.
    Hold the word that hurts.
    Kindness speaks through silence.

This year I wear his hat,
feel his touch inside his coat.
Inside my voice he speaks
of what it means to be.
He loved with what he was.

Mingo Junction—December 2014
for Guy Mason

I walk down the morning hill
past the blank faced houses
leaning in the wind
to visit an old friend
And together we walk the
streets of our hometown—
past dark storefronts, cold as glass.

We talk the weather of memories
Beyond the orange of mill gate steps
we enter the Towne House bar—
cozy quarters for home folks,
a juke box of country tunes,
old oak bar along the wall.
We meet faces of the past
warn and warm, and I nod
as my friend connects the names.
Hands go out across the years.

We sit with our eggs and toast
bring coffee to our lips
and our words go back and forth
between today and then—
stories of classmates, thoughts of politics,
the way the world keeps going wrong,
things we hold on to.

Back on the streets
we walk to Minch's.
My friend opens the front door
to a room full of men my father's age.
"Hey, ain't you Deb Smith's boy?
Your old man worked the rails in Weirton,"

they ask and answer. I nod,
shake hands again and again
with these storytellers of my town.

Then we enter the "back room,"
where men my age—retired or laid off—
read my face, think memory.
"Smitty, yeah, how's your brother?"
"Okay, and how's your Mom?"
In a while the play will begin,
cards slapped down,
chips cast out, drawn in.
It is a rite as old as men and this town.

We stand around, then say so long,
duck out the door. Snow is falling lightly
in the streets of our mill town
and this story of friends
after all these years.

Ohio Valley—Business as Usual

A dog barks in a neighbor's yard while the garbage truck pulls up the alley. Sun is beaming off the white vinyl siding as cars rush up and down the hill. It takes a certain momentum to go anywhere around here.

Last night Ralph the furnace man came over at 9 pm to check my mother-in-law's air conditioner. I held the flashlight, listened to Ralph, then offered him a cup of coffee.

This morning my wife and Sue have gone off to have their hair 'done.' at Jeanette's Beauty Shop down on Commercial Avenue.

The backs of those buildings face the railroad tracks that run along the river. I've seen them from inside the mill as trains pulled ladles of hot slag and liquid steel alongside the huge blast furnaces. "Dinosaurs" they call them now. The roar and clash of it all is almost too much. Smoke rises to the pale skies; a flame torches the excess gas overhead. It's continuous cast operation—a century of working round the clock in shifts.

On the hills are nested red brick schools, raising our children to something more, another kind of labor, lifting with the mind.

Outside my window, mill-gray pigeons perch on power lines.

Cutting Down the Maple in My Father's Yard

It is the day after Thanksgiving and we walk out in morning air. The leaves have already gone. My father is showing me how the bark has come away from the trunk. It clearly can't be saved. So, we bring ladders up from the garage, my brother's chainsaw out from the basement.

As I hold this ladder for my father, my son runs about the yard chasing their old dog. I see it is a 62-year-old man up there cutting branches which fall at my feet, and there is this unspeakable sadness. Why do I allow him to do it? Because I want him young, and yet I fear his loss. I am on a ladder myself holding him.

My father offers me the noisy saw. I shy away. "No, go ahead and cut," I say. He holds it out again and nods, "You'll need to know this soon enough." But I let him cut. "I'll gather up," I say, and I remember all the times I've worked with him, the lights and tools I've passed along. I've come to love his act of work, the surest thing I know.

I catch the logs as they fall from his saw and stack them near the garage. My son drags the thin branches down the yard. And soon our arms grow warm with work. There is no need to talk. We speak in acts, the light inside the yard.

In the sunny rhythm of our working I think....*How did this man, my father, become so easily old?* I want my son to know this man. I want this job to never end. I will ache for weeks with the rightness of this work.

Where I Am Going/ Where I Have Been
A Dream Poem

Outside the mill gate
I wait for my dead father
to come out .

He will raise his arm
in salute to the fifteen years
since we last spoke.

He will be wearing his brakeman's clothes
dark jacket and pants shedding dirt,
his work gloves folded in his cap.

And I will glide the car forward
wave to his tired but smiling face,
and he will open the door and get in.

Wordless we will drive along the river
the road so familiar,
the car's engine the only voice.

At the traffic light before the bridge
we will read each other's faces,
touch the space inside our hearts.

His hands will be rough and
read like a road map
all the way home.

Visiting My Sister Alone in Winter

She opens the door of her little house:
three dogs lick the snow from my boots.
I set down my bags, offer her a bottle of wine.
She has prepared a casserole and bread.

"Do my sixty years show on my face," I ask;
"Ha," she laughs, "I'm nearly fifty myself."
For a moment we grow silent—
our dead parents pass through the room.

They lie on a hill not far from here
alone together above their old town.
And so, we each have our lives—
I—my books and words, she—her house and dogs.

Mates and children have filled us too.
We sit at table, cast lines across the years,
hoping to pull ourselves together,
two boats mooring along the shore.

Climbing the Knob Through Trees
in Early Spring

The way up the hill leads through the trees
spread out like a farm of wilderness.

As a boy I walked here with friends
finding the path through green weeds
till we came to the tall spreading oak,
its tire swing hanging from a cable.
Someone would grab the rope and pull it back,
then swing out over the valley stream—
our breath held full in our chest
till we let it out in a yell for life.

One by one we would drop off
into the waiting stream, bathed in sun.

A man of sixty now,
with my own children grown,
loving wife at home,
I sit on this rock in leafy shade
stare at the thin trunk of a maple
that becomes my own thoughts.
And the sunlight through leaves
is the way beyond words.

Sunday Service in the Ohio Valley

I stand in cemetery snow
one foot on each grave:
my father—my mother, to ask
forgiveness, announce great grandchildren
they would love and somehow
already know.

I drive to their old church,
enter smiling and penitent,
greeted by smiling children and
take the chubby hands of elders.
The church attendance is as sparse
as a winter garden, so I sing stronger
to keep the tunes alive. Up the aisle
comes my aging aunt in the choir,
nodding to me and to life.

Two days ago I stood at the edge of town
looking down at the abandoned stadium
a ruined school bus in a field of snow,
the lights of the mill without sound,
freight cars dead on their tracks.
Wearing a coat of loss, I turned,
walked back into town, and stood
at the Catholic schoolyard watching
children glide over fresh snow tracks.

There and then I sought to surrender
bridging past to present, placing
the old memory stick on the shelf.
And I said to myself again and again:
"What was—was, and what is—is,"
My eyes and heart were bound in this chorus
till I knew at last I could not follow it,

that to stop this 'going' home, I must simply
'be' at home and share the stories being told.

Back at the church recessional, I wake
to words flowing from my lips:

> "Let there be peace on earth,
> And let it begin with me."

In the parking lot, I close my aunt's car door,
and sparrows rise to blue snowy skies.

Pesta's Country Store since 1942

Larry Smith is a native of the industrial Ohio River Valley having grown up in Mingo Junction, Ohio., the second of four children. His father was a brakeman on the railroad of Weirton Steel where the author worked two summers to help pay for college. A graduate of Mingo High School (1961), Muskingum College (1965), and Kent State University (1974),  he taught at Bowling Green State University's Firelands College from 1970 to 2012. He married hometown girl, Ann (Zaben) Smith in 1965 when they moved to Euclid, Ohio to start long careers in teaching and in nursing.

He is the author of eight previous books of poetry, two books of memoirs, five books of fiction, two literary biographies of authors Lawrence Ferlinghetti and Kenneth Patchen, and two books of poetry translations from the Chinese. Smith has received fellowships from the Ohio Arts Council and the National Endowment for the Humanities and was a Fulbright Lecturer in Italy from 1980 to 1981.

His photo history of hometown Mingo Junction, Ohio co-edited with Guy Mason appeared in Arcadia's Images of America Series. Two of his film scripts on authors James Wright and Kenneth Patchen have been made into films with his co-director Tom Koba. He was the first poet laureate of Huron, Ohio.

Larry is the founder and director of The Firelands Writing Center and Bottom Dog Press and co-founder with his wife, Ann, of Converging Paths Meditation Center in Huron, Ohio. He and his wife live along the sandy shores of Lake Erie in Huron, Ohio, and are parents of three adults and eight grandchildren.

Construction of Mingo City Building 1955 and
book cover of *Images of America, Mingo Junction*

BOOKS BY BOTTOM DOG PRESS
Harmony Series

The Pears by Larry Smith 62 pgs. $12

Without a Plea by Jeff Gundy 96 pgs. $16

What Burden Do Those Trains Bear Away, by Kathleen S. Burgess 96 pgs. $16

Taking a Walk in My Animal Hat, by Charlene Fix, 90 pgs, $16

Earnest Occupations, by Richard Hague, 200 pgs, $18

Pieces: A Composite Novel, by Mary Ann McGuigan, 250 pgs, $18

Crows in the Jukebox: Poems, by Mike James, 106 pgs, $16

Portrait of the Artist as a Bingo Worker: by Lori Jakiela, 216 pgs, $18

The Thick of Thin: A Memoir, by Larry Smith, 238 pgs, $18

Cold Air Return: Novel, by Patrick Lawrence O'Keeffe, 390 pgs, $20

Flesh and Stones: A Memoir, by Jan Shoemaker, 176 pgs, $18

Waiting to Begin: A Memoir by Patricia O'Donnell, 166 pgs, $18

And Waking: Poems by Kevin Casey, 80 pgs, $16

Both Shoes Off: Poems by Jeanne Bryner, 112 pgs, $16

Abandoned Homeland: Poems by Jeff Gundy, 96 pgs, $16

Stolen Child: A Novel by Suzanne Kelly, 338 pgs, $18

On the Flyleaf: Poems by Herbert Woodward Martin, 106 pgs, $16

The Harmonist at Nightfall: Poems by Shari Wagner, 114 pgs, $16

Painting Bridges: A Novel by Patricia Averbach, 234 pgs, $18

Ariadne & Other Poems by Ingrid Swanberg, 120 pgs, $16

The Search for the Reason Why: Poems by Tom Kryss, 192 pgs, $16

Kenneth Patchen: Rebel Poet in America by Larry Smith, Revised 2nd Edition, 326 pgs, Cloth $28

Selected Correspondence of Kenneth Patchen, Edited with introduction by Allen Frost, Paper $18/ Cloth $28

Awash with Roses: Collected Love Poems of Kenneth Patchen Eds. Laura Smith and Larry Smith 200 pgs, $16

Breathing the West: Poems by Liane Ellison Norman, 96 pgs, $16

Maggot: A Novel by Robert Flanagan, 262 pgs, $18

American Poet: A Novel by Jeff Vande Zande, 200 pgs, $18

The Way-Back Room: Memoir of a Detroit Childhood by Mary Minock, 216 pgs, $18

Echo: Poems by Christina Lovin 86 pgs. $16

Bottom Dog Press http://smithdocs.net

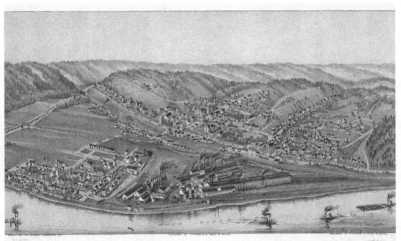

MINGO JUNCTION.

CPSIA information can be obtained
at www.ICGtesting.com
Printed in the USA
FSHW011124280920
74178FS